TOO GOOD TO LOSE

A Competency-Based, Dual-Track
Employee Development Solution
To Help Companies Keep Good People

Bloom and Maslow Unite To Organize Your Business, Engage & Retain Your Top Talent

By
Todd J. Lemmis, JD

Copyright 2021 by Todd J Lemmis, JD – All Rights Reserved.

It is not legal to reproduce, duplicate or transmit any part of this document in either electronic means or written format. Recording of this publication is strictly prohibited.

This book is dedicated to:

All my former bosses who showed me what to do and, equally as important, what not to do.

Table of Contents

Introduction 1
PART I: How Companies Work and The Mistakes They Make 10
    Chapter One: How Companies Work .. 10
    Chapter Two: 3 Mistakes Companies Make and the Horrible Things They Do to Try to Correct Them 16
PART II: The Solution 24
    Chapter Three: Meet the Players: Bloom & Maslow 25
    Chapter Four: Introduction to Competencies 35
    Chapter Five: The Four Competencies 40
    Chapter Six: Meet Your New Best Friends: The Job Description & The Org Chart 52
    Chapter Seven: Back to the Beginning – Hire the Right People 64
Epilogue/Conclusion 68
Acknowledgments 69
About the Author 70

"Success is not the key to happiness. Happiness is the key to success. If you love what you are doing, you will be successful."

-Albert Schweitzer

Introduction

My name is Todd Lemmis, and I can't thank you enough for purchasing my little book. You probably don't know it yet, but you've just taken the first step to simplifying your HR life and transforming your company into a happier, healthier and better organization. The book may be relatively small, but it contains some pretty big ideas that will help you and your organization enormously.

Whether you're an HR professional, a senior leader or a business owner, the following pages will highlight what most companies do wrong and open your eyes to a new way of viewing your most important company assets: your employees. The model that follows was proven effective during my tenure as CHRO of a Fortune 150 company. I'm not a lifelong HR professional, and I consider this a plus, as most companies seem to make the same mistakes over and over. When dealing with people, a little common sense, science, psychology, diversity of experience and a fresh set of objective eyes go a long way to inspire innovation and improvement of tired old models and practices.

Since you bought the book, I figure you might like to know a little about the author. I won't bore you with too many details, but the employment journey that brought me to penning this little project was a fairly long and schizophrenic one, and the explanation will at least partially explain why I decided to share my past frustrations that grew in the HR dual track, competency-based career development model that follows.

I grew up in Barrington, Rhode Island, USA in the 1970's and started working as soon as I was able. I had a paper route with my best friend Jeff who moved to England, and when I was old enough, I worked as a service clerk at grocery stores, and had a brief stint flipping burgers for a chain that will remain nameless (but involved royalty). On my first day at the grocery store, my dad gave me the following piece of advice, "the boss isn't always right, but he's always the boss". That stuck with me, and in the 40+ years that followed that summer of 1979 I've been fortunate enough to learn from a great many bosses, some wonderful, others painfully horrible.

At age 12, I started playing the saxophone and got pretty good pretty fast, so I started working in bands, which led me to a four-year tour of duty performing with the US Navy Band, where

I was stationed at Naval Station, Pearl Harbor Hawaii.

At the end of my tour, I moved to California to live with my brother and attend college. While at UCLA pursuing a degree in philosophy, I worked as a suit salesman, a waiter, a bartender/bar manager and as assistant security director for the UCLA student stores, where I stayed-on after graduation, until a dear friend and mentor, Malibu attorney Bob Ferguson, changed my life path by convincing me to go to law school.

While in law school, I tended bar for the first year and then got a job working as a clerk for a hilarious, larger-than-life Irish American attorney who remarkably did not enjoy the practice of law. So as a second-year law student I was left to handle a fairly sizeable civil law practice (mostly business and personal injury cases) while my boss partied, spray painted his quickly receding scalp, chased younger women and did a little criminal defense work on the side. I regretfully extricated him from a malpractice suit by drafting a particularly creative legal demurrer, then promptly resigned and went to work for the State Bar of California, which esteemed entity, in its infinite wisdom, rescinded his license to practice law shortly thereafter.

While studying for the bar exam, Mr. Ferguson put me to work on the used car lot of a Santa Monica luxury automobile dealership (where he served as VP and general counsel) that was frequented by a great number of Hollywood celebrities. I once spent one glorious summer afternoon smoking cigarettes with Sean Penn while he entertained me with endless stories about boxing, and another being ignored by J-Lo (who asked all of her questions by whispering to a member of her entourage who, in turn, relayed the questions to me). I was relentlessly teased on a regular basis by the late great comedian George Carlin (my absolute favorite customer).

While waiting for my bar exam results, I moved to the new car lot and upon receiving my passing results, my friend informed me that "practicing law is no way to make a living, kid", and I was immediately promoted to the position of finance manager and shortly thereafter to sales manager. During my time at the dealership, I learned a great deal about how businesses run, how to manage and, more importantly, how *not* to manage people.

After one spectacularly horrible, humiliating, hilarious senior leadership meeting with the owner of the dealership, I apologized to my friend, quit my job and got a job in Inglewood helping to run a motorcycle dealership (more on my lessons at the car dealership later on).

After figuring out how motorcycle stores operated (most dealers rip people off, by the way), I did a little math, changed the pricing and advertising strategy to one of complete honesty, and the store went from selling 15 bikes per week to 100.

The owner bought a Kawasaki shop in Orange County and we improved the store's standing from number 1450 of 1500 dealers nationally to number 9 in the nation in as many months.

Then 2009 happened, the housing market crashed, customers stopped coming-in with their home equity loan checks, and the motorcycle finance market tightened-up like a revolutionary war snare drum. The owner's son, with a fresh MBA and no business experience whatsoever, had recently bought every failing dealership on the west coast that he could get his hands on and completely depleted the company's capital. We were sunk.

Fortunately, my dear friend (and now business partner) John Molina, who at the time was running Molina Healthcare with his physician brother Mario, said he needed some help in HR and thought I might be a good fit.

The company had no HR positions available, so, being a lawyer, they started me in the legal department doing a complete refresh of the company's universe of job descriptions with an emphasis on FLSA exemption status (a great way to get to know how a company works, by the way – go through a company's org chart and review all the job descriptions and you'll quickly see who does what and why).

After realizing I had a knack for people and HR, and absolutely no interest in practicing law in the exciting field of Medicaid managed care, I was asked to take over the struggling recruiting department.

After a few weeks, I figured-out how recruiting departments work and started to find ways to improve the operation. They were using lots of agencies (are recruiters really supposed to do nothing but manage outside agencies?) and hiring the majority of mid-levels and executives from outside the company (where were the internal promotions?). I also starting to measure things like fill rate and turnover and discovered that it was taking way too long to fill positions and far too many employees were quitting to work elsewhere.

My HR research showed that it should reasonably take about a month to fill a vacant position, and we had a fill rate nearly twice that. Hiring managers were not happy.

The agency spend was far too high, and I also discovered that some placement agencies had been spending far too much time hanging around inside our company, schmoozing hiring managers, bringing gifts, buying lunches, etc. I put an end to that ridiculous practice immediately, then started having regular meetings with department heads and convinced them to give in-house recruiting a chance.

My research also showed that a company's *total* turnover (including terminations) should be under 20%, and that our *voluntary* turnover rate was well over 20%. Good people were leaving. Something was clearly wrong.

Long story short (this isn't a book about recruiting), we quickly got recruiting flowing as it should, earning the trust and confidence of senior leadership and for some inexplicable reason I was made head of HR.

I now had Recruiting, Training & Development, Employee Relations, Total Rewards, HR Systems, Work Comp/Safety, Diversity & Inclusion and Policies & Procedures under me – all the pieces of the puzzle needed to figure out and fix the steadily increasing employee turnover problem.

I was having a chat one afternoon with our company psychologist, the late great Dr. Larry Lewis (who spent his early career touring with famous rock bands, charged with keeping them sober in order to fulfill their contractual obligations). We were discussing Bloom's taxonomy of learning and BINGO! I had an epiphany – combine Bloom's levels to mastery with Maslow's hierarchy of needs and you get both sides of the employee equation: Levels of skill/career progression and what the workplace must provide to fulfill their needs and therefore fuel their progression. And that's where our story begins…but first, I'd like to share a brief word on consultants, if I may.

I've learned many important lessons in my career, and hopefully you can learn from this and not make the same mistake that many do…DON'T WASTE YOUR COMPANY'S MONEY ON CONSULTANTS! (I'm generally not a fan of all caps, but I'll make an exception here). Here's everything I know about consultants: 1. They have one mission: to extend the pendency of their consulting contract as long as possible, thereby taking as much money from you as they possibly can. To achieve this, they make simple concepts and processes needlessly complicated; and 2. Generally, these "experts" do not know any more about their subject matter than you do.

Finally, I wrote this book mindful of Occam's Razor. I'm sure that most of you know it. It states, "entities should not be multiplied without necessity", or more simply put, "the simplest explanation is usually the correct one". I promise you that by the time you finish this short book, you will learn the mistakes that companies make and how to avoid them, why good people leave, how to prevent many of them from leaving, improve your company's morale and culture by showing them that they have a clear career path and opportunity for promotion. You'll have a simple way to overcome the needlessly complicated game of job competencies, job descriptions and career paths. I'll provide virtually all the tools you'll need - there are a few company and job specific things you'll have to insert (I don't know your business) to create useful job descriptions and career paths for your most valuable assets, your employees. Your retention will go up – your recruiting and replacement costs will go down.

Like you, I hate reading long business books that don't get to the point fast, so I'll make you another promise – I'll keep the chapters short and to the point. Each will end with the most important takeaways and build on the previous chapter so the whole thing will make sense in the end. Now turn the page and let's get started reading Part I, which describes the basics of how companies work and the avoidable mistakes they make.

PART I: Companies and the Mistakes They Make

Chapter One: How Companies Work

I know the information in this first chapter will seem rudimentary and obvious to the vast majority of people, but it will get us all on the same page and set a solid base of understanding for us to build upon together. So please know that I don't mean to insult the reader's intelligence, but this stuff is important. Here we go…

Let's first ask ourselves *what is a company*? There are countless ways to describe one, but I'm going to go with a simple and intuitive definition. **A company is a group of people organized (that's why they call them *organizations*) to get something done.**

Three parts: People. Organization. Mission.

Neither this book nor your organization will be successful if we don't remember to focus on all three parts. An overused three-legged stool reference comes to mind (that such a stool will fail without all three legs), but I won't use it (darn it, I just did…apologies). All three parts are equally important, but, as my dad used to say, "everybody's equal, but some are more equal than others". Point is, while all three parts are *technically* equal, the *people* part is more equal than the other two.

You can invent noble, cool and innovative missions all day long, and design org charts and production flow charts until the cows come home, but you can accomplish nothing without PEOPLE. Unfortunately, people are messy. They have moods. They call in sick. They don't always get along. They are competitive. They are lazy. They need to eat and sleep and poop and cry and celebrate and feel and love. They need to be loved and nurtured and hugged and thanked and corrected and paid and praised and comforted and sometimes fired. They do great things, creative things, stupid things, dangerous things and brilliant things. I could go on and on, but bottom line, people are a glorious pain in the ass. Sorry folks, it's what and who we have to work with.

People need stuff to do. To do stuff they need to be organized. You can't pursue a mission without people. Organized people.

To accomplish their mission, most companies spend more time focusing on the organizing part than the people part. I'm going to help you with the people part, for people are my species and I like to help people. Let's see how people fit into organizations.

Nearly all organizations are set up in the same basic manner. It looks like the side of a pyramid – a big triangle with levels inside it. For right now, let's keep it simple and make it three levels:

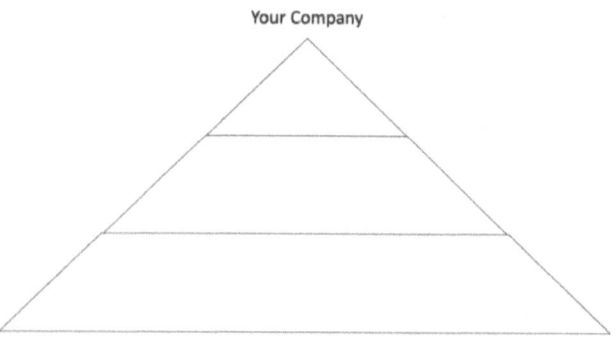

There are lots of people in the bottom level, fewer in the middle level and very few on the top.

There are lots of easy jobs, fewer pretty hard jobs and very few really hard jobs.

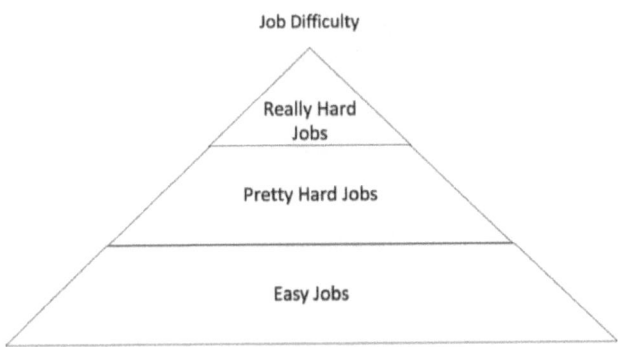

Most people are led by others, managed by some more, and led by a few at the top – the folks at the top generate the company's mission.

The hoards at the bottom are easy to find. It's harder to find the ones in the middle and the

folks are as hard to find as a purple squirrel.

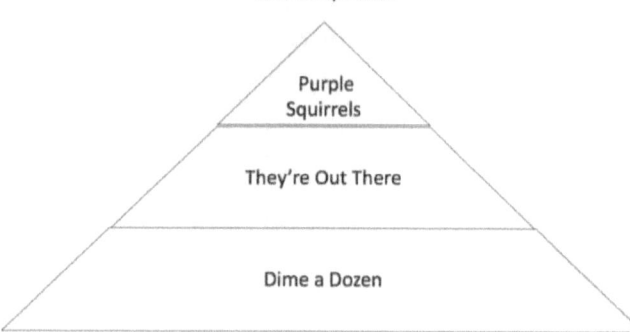

Companies have bunches of cheap employees, fewer mid-priced employees and very few really expensive employees.

Most of the less expensive folks at the bottom are fairly new and thus not fully indoctrinated into the company's culture and core values. The ones in the middle tend to have more tenure and better model the culture and values. The few at the top generate and embody the culture and values.

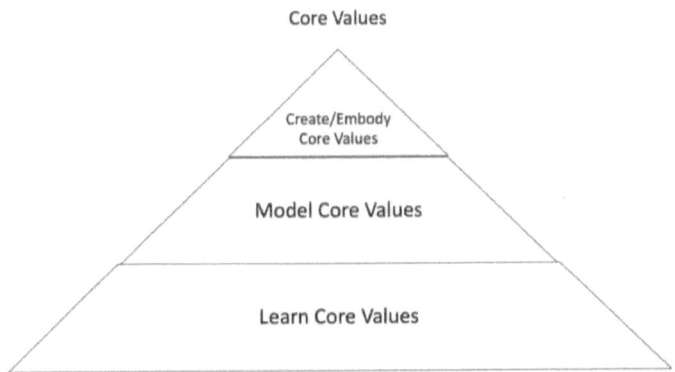

Here's the interesting part. As we move up the levels of the corporate pyramid, we have fewer and fewer people, and those fewer and fewer people have an increasingly larger and larger impact on the company's culture, employees and performance.

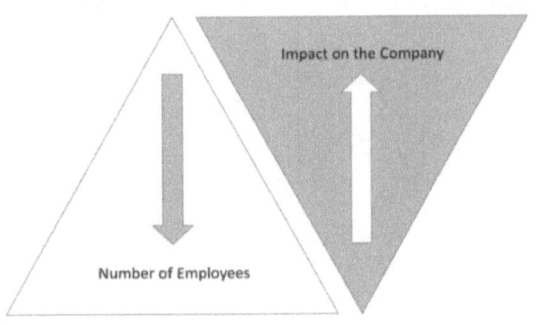

As you'll see a little later, this can be a good thing or a bad thing.

Chapter Summary/Key Takeaways

- Companies are shaped like pyramids

- There are lots of cheap, easy to find employees on the bottom with the simplest jobs

- There are very few really expensive, hard to find people on the top with all the power and influence

In the next chapter, you'll learn the mistakes companies often make in this model.

Chapter Two: 3 Mistakes Companies Make and the Horrible Things They Do to Try to Correct Them

While the traditional pyramid model generally works well, the system breaks down when the masses at the bottom don't stay and grow with the company to become the middle folks and the top folks. The outflow of good, culturally compatible employees with growth potential and the goofy ways companies try to keep them can seriously sabotage the health and success of the company in general.

In my career I've seen it all. People shoehorned into the wrong job description in an attempt to properly compensate them at the correct level. Brilliant misanthrope individual contributors being promoted into leadership positions in order to retain them and their highly valuable skill set. The highly creative invention of novel, non-ratable job titles curated for individuals to make them happy and retain their services. All completely wrong and a lesson to be learned from each.

We know these truths to be self-evident: That good employees leave the company. That these folks are often replaced with outsiders. That companies try to combat the outflow of good employees by doing some pretty stupid (and sometimes shady) ways. Let's take a look at each of these in turn.

Mistake 1: Letting Good Employees Leave

During my time in corporate America, I observed many fine people leaving my company. The lower-level employees often left for a buck or two more per hour in pay – a normal sort of event that can't easily be overcome (but perhaps it can be curtailed – more to follow when we get to career pathing). Most companies accept and live with this fact because these employees are fairly inexpensive to recruit, train and pay.

What became more concerning to me was the increasing number of mid-level employees leaving the company. After resuscitating the company's exit interview program, the answer became clear. Mid-level *individual contributors*, many of whom were IT folks, engineers and other technical folks, represented the vast majority of those fleeing the company.

When asked why they were leaving, a great many of them cited two reasons. The first reason was…wait for it…better job titles! Yes –

they were leaving not because they were dissatisfied with their boss or their position or their salary, but because the job title at the new company was more prestigious sounding, often with false supervisory, management and leadership titles, even though the positions had no direct reports.

The other reason sounded much more reasonable. They said they believed the new company had better prospects for promotion and career growth. So there it was, in black and white. Mid-level employees were dropping our company like a dirty shirt because we weren't sufficiently showing them that they had a promising future at our company.

Keep reading until Part 2 and I'll give you the solution, BUT DON'T SKIP AHEAD!

Mistake 2: Replacing Middle Management/Executives Using Agencies

While reviewing the company's recruiting data, I also noticed, as I mentioned in the introduction, that a disproportionate number of mid-level and executive level vacancies were being filled by professional placement agencies. For the mid-level positions, these highly predatory firms were infiltrating our company, buddying-up with, gifting, wining and dining our hiring managers. As crazy as this sounds, they were even doing it in our recruiting department.

Here's how they worked – they'd review our job postings on the job sites. At the time, they were Monster, Indeed, LinkedIn and other field-specific specialty sites. They'd see what positions were open and convince (bribe, cajole, pay, trade) the hiring manager that they had the perfect candidate, just waiting to go. They'd even offer them as temps (for which they'd get commission) so the managers could try them out prior to hiring them (another, larger commission). With this kind of influence being exerted upon the hiring managers, our in-house recruiters didn't stand a chance – often, they weren't even given the opportunity to present candidates to the hiring managers. Needless to say, I put an end to that unfair and extremely expensive practice.

To make matters worse, the departing mid-levels had been fully acculturated to our company and they were being replaced by people who had to be indoctrinated to our company's culture from scratch. It was a revolving door of newbies unnecessarily replacing perfectly good, high quality, productive employees.

When mid-level employees leave because they perceive 1) their job title as insufficiently prestigious, 2) their prospects for promotion and growth are low, and they are replaced by outsiders instead of internal candidates seeking promotion, you know you have a problem.

The other problem, as I stated earlier, was that executive vacancies were also being filled at an alarming rate by executive placement agencies at great expense. This happens for two reasons.

Firstly, the C-Suite had no faith in the ability of the recruiting department to fill executive-level positions. I can't say that I blame them. The department had two "executive recruiters" that spent most of their time schmoozing the existing executives instead of searching the web and contacting other companies to find interested candidates. And they were only too happy to accommodate the C-Suite hiring manager requests to engage executive search firms, many of which were retained and extremely expensive. Why waste all that energy looking for candidates when all you had to do is make one call to Heidrick & Struggles, sit back and wait for the high-end luxury candidates to be presented.

Secondly, the company had no succession planning program whatsoever. Thus, there were no internal candidates being groomed and prepared to replace the company's aging executives. I put such a succession planning program in place (a very simple and effective one, If I do say so myself, but that's another book I have yet to write) and that, along with earning the C-Suite's confidence, went a long way to solve this problem of filling a disproportionate number of executive positions with external hires.

As we'll see next, the incorrect solution only compounds the problem for the company.

Mistake 3: Retention by Improper Title/Promotion and Unnecessary Layering of Extra Levels

In an effort to retain either good employees (or hook-up their brother-in-law, see below), managers, many of whom were in IT, started a couple of practices that took me some time to catch-on to.

Scenario: a manager has an employee who happens to be an individual contributor that they want to keep after they learn the employee has wanderlust and/or an earnest desire for a more prestigious title or promotion/career opportunity. There are currently no higher-level open positions to which to promote the employee, either because all the higher positions are filled or the employee has topped-out in his/her career path, so the manager feels that (s)he has no choice but to get creative.

First creative choice for what to do with the employee: promote the employee into an open management role even though the employee is neither interested in becoming, or qualified to become, a people manager. You want to keep the employee, so you make him/her a manager, effectively pulling him/her off their professional track and putting him or her on a (wrong) management career track. The poor person now has direct reports the (s)he has no idea how to manage and will make both him/herself miserable along with all the people (s)he is now managing poorly – ruining the morale of perfectly good employees.

Equally as bad is the scenario where the employee has topped-out in his/her individual contributor/professional job track and the *only* way to reward him/her is to promote him/her into a management position (or lose the employee). Back when I was in the car business, an *old timer* in the business taught me an important lesson that had an enormous impact and has stuck with me to this day, He said, "never make your best salesman the manager, kid".

Those words are so true and always occupy the back of my mind. The skill set that makes someone an amazing salesperson (mainly greed and self-interest) is completely different from the skill set that makes one an amazing manager (caring for others, team building and the heartfelt desire to see others grow and succeed). Rewarding a star individual contributor with a management position is like rewarding a baby with chainsaw – they'll be frustrated, and they won't know what to do with it, and if they try to use it they'll probably do an enormous amount of damage.

The second choice managers have under this scenario is just as bad, and maybe worse: Invent a title/position (either a management or individual contributor title) and slot the new title/position in between two existing levels. This ridiculous practice is often exposed with the word "senior". Example: You have supervisor that is qualified for promotion and should be made a manager, but there are no manager positions open. You fear losing the employee, so you invent the title "senior supervisor" or "supervisor 2" or anything to make it look like a promotion.

In this second scenario, you end up with a department or company with so many layers it looks like one of those cakes you get at the

Claim Jumper and regret immediately thereafter. You have workers reporting to leads reporting to supervisors reporting to senior supervisors reporting to managers reporting to senior managers reporting directors reporting to senior directors reporting AVP's reporting to VP's reporting to Senior VP's reporting EVP's…that's 12 (count 'em…12) levels of reporting. And the poor bottom level worker is the only one doing any productive work! This is the exact situation I encountered at my company.

Is there a solution to this stuff? Absolutely! You'll find it in Part 2, which you are about to turn to. But first, here's a fun one…

A criminally fun situation: the infamous *brother-in-law* scenario! A manager in the other (brother-in-law) scenario, would make a deal with another manager that would go something like this: One agrees to hire an unqualified relative or friend of the other manager in a low-level position - keep him/her around for a few months and then do an internal transfer to a higher level, usually management position in the other department after significantly padding the brother-in-law's resume and basically doing an end run around the recruiting department. You do it for my cousin now, and next month I'll do it for your wife's nephew. I include this mostly for fun and to remind you that "ya gotta watch these guys!!"

Chapter Summary/Key Takeaways

- Companies often lose great mid-level employees for something completely preventable: an erroneous perception by the employee that they'll have more prestige and upward mobility elsewhere

- Companies often replace mid-level employees and executives with external hires because of lack of trust in the recruiting department and perks from predatory agencies, killing morale and filling the company with the unacculturated.

- Companies often promote individual contributors into management positions to retain the employee which makes them and their employees miserable or invent new titles/positions to promote employees when there are currently no open higher positions, resulting in far too many levels in the company.

In the Part II, we will solve all the problems we just described, and thereby make you a hero at your company.

PART II: The Solution

In Part I, we looked at the hierarchical, pyramidal manner in which companies are organized, and how such a system can break down if disenchanted employees leave and are replaced by outsiders, resulting in more disenchanted employees, too many levels and an unsustainable, ever changing company culture.

As promised, Part II will offer you a simple, science-based solution for how to build competency-based job descriptions, visible career paths that make sense, allowing growth and progression without making brilliant individual contributors become managers, relatively flat org charts that make sense, and what stuff you need to feed your employees so they can happily progress up your company ladder without wanting to flee.

But first, let's meet a couple of dead guys that will help us along the way…Messrs. Bloom and Maslow.

Chapter Three: Meet the Players: Bloom & Maslow

Benjamin Bloom: The Tree

Apologies, reader, for the goofy metaphor, but it's a pretty easy way to look at the model. Bloom is the tree (get it? *Bloom*?) and Maslow's going to be the water. People in jobs bloom and grow if they are watered properly. It's understandable and just makes sense.
Okay…let's talk about ol' Ben Bloom, or better yet, let's let Wikipedia talk about him…

"Benjamin Samuel Bloom (2/21/13 - 9/13/99) was an American educational psychologist who made contributions to the classification of educational objectives and to the theory of *mastery learning*. He is particularly noted for leading educational psychologists to develop the comprehensive system of describing and assessing educational outcomes in the mid-1950's. He has influenced the practices and philosophies of educators around the world from the latter part of the twentieth century.

In 1956, Bloom edited the first volume of *The Taxonomy of Educational Objectives: The Classification of Educational Goals*, which classified learning objectives according to a rubric that has come to be known as *Bloom's Taxonomy*. It was one of the first attempts to systematically classify levels of cognitive functioning and gave structure to the otherwise amorphous mental processes of gifted students." (Wikipedia)

What does all this mean? Let's cut to the chase – In practical (musically metaphorical – sorry, I started my career as a musician) terms, *Bloom's Taxonomy* say you need to learn and master your scales before you can play Mary Had a Little Lamb. You need to master Mary Had a Little Lamb before you can play Beethoven's Sonata. You need to master Beethoven's Sonata before you understand how Beethoven composed his Sonata. You need to master the understanding of how the Sonata fits in with Beethoven's other music, and you need to master the understanding of Beethoven's library of music before you can write your own Beethoven-like sonata.

In essence, you need to learn to master walking before you can start running. Here an illustration of Dr. Bloom's levels:

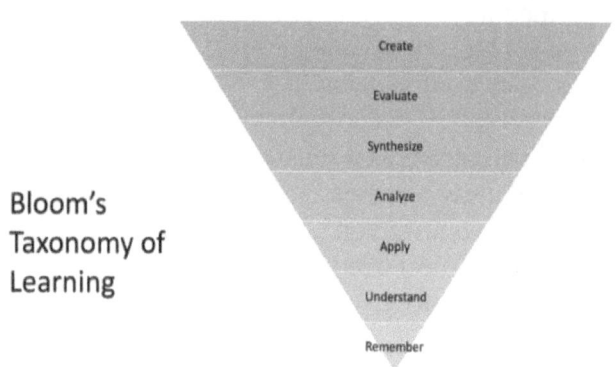

Hint: the fact that the pyramid has seven levels is significant.[1]

I made this an upside-down pyramid to make a couple of points. First, the easiest (small) stuff is on the bottom – you have to master the little, easy things before you move up to the next level, prepared to learn to master more difficult

---

[1] Originally, Bloom's system had only six levels (omitting *synthesize)*, but modernly, the truly astute agree that seven levels is the way to go.

(larger) tasks. Second, please note the parallel to the increasing impact on the organization that the performance of the increasingly more difficult tasks has.

Let's view this from an organizational perspective. The newer, culturally-uninitiated, lower paid employees with the least experience are assigned the easiest, more rote tasks. They have to master those tasks before they can handle more complicated ones. And so-on and so-forth.

Bloom's levels to mastery and the definitions we'll be using are as follows:

1. Remember: the ability to recall, copy and imitate

2. Understand: the ability to follow, comprehend and interpret instructions

3. Apply: the ability to execute independently and reliably in response to real circumstances

4. Analyze: the ability to interpret and integrate elements, principles and relationships

5. Synthesize: the ability to autonomously combine elements and principles to

contribute to and improve new systems and models

6. Evaluate: the ability to see how systems and models contribute to the enterprise in order to create, develop and improve new systems and models

7. Create: the ability to generate novel concepts that empower the enterprise

Later on, we'll see how these seven levels fit-in to job descriptions, career paths and corporate structure, but for now, it's well enough that you just know and understand them. Let's move on to Dr. Maslow.

Abraham Maslow: The Water

So, if Bloom's the tree which grows bigger and stronger, guess who the water is? Ready for it? You got it! Abraham Maslow[2]. Here's what our friends at Wikipedia have to say about Abe:

"Abraham Harold Maslow (4/1/08 - 6/8/70) was an American psychologist who was best known for creating *Maslow's Hierarchy of Needs*, a theory of psychological health predicated on

---

[2] Please take note that I call Maslow the water and not the fertilizer, which would be a horrible, unfair, unkind and likely illegal use of metaphor.

fulfilling innate human needs in priority, culminating self-actualization…He stressed the importance of focusing on the positive qualities in people, as opposed to treating them as 'a bag of symptoms'".

The father of *humanistic psychology*, Maslow felt that the ultimate goal of living is to attain personal growth and understanding through constant self-improvement, and that peoples most basic needs must be met as a prerequisite to achieving higher levels of mastery and ultimately self-actualization. He was a really positive, optimistic guy!

Let's look at Dr. Maslow's pyramid:

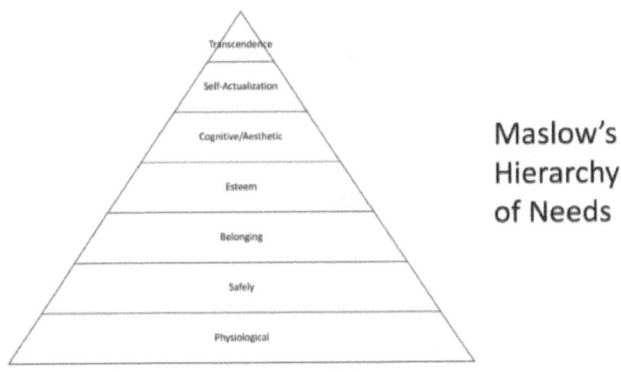

Maslow's Hierarchy of Needs

This pyramid is not inverted to illustrate the parallel to the number of people that occupy the different levels of an organization and the relative level difficulty of satisfying each progressive need. *Another spoiler alert: Maslow's pyramid ALSO has seven levels.*[3]

Here are Maslow's levels and how we'll define them:

1. Physiological: the need for nutrition, hydration, shelter and a bathroom

2. Safety: the need for security of body, health, employment, resources and morality

3. Belonging: the need for friendship, a work family and someone in whom one can confide

4. Esteem: the need to feel respected by and have respect for others, confidence, achievement and upward mobility

---

[3] Maslow's levels can vary from six to eight – some psychologists either split or omit *cognitive and aesthetic* and others omit *transcendence*, but for business organizations, I find that seven levels work best.

5. Cognitive/Aesthetic: the need to feel one has deep organizational understanding and to get the big picture

6. Self-Actualization: empowerment, self-knowledge, creativity, morality, problem solving and justice

7. Transcendence: visionary intuition, altruism, unity consciousness and perspective of where the organization fits into the outside world

As we see in the pyramid above, Maslow teaches us that our physiological needs must be met as a prerequisite to our feeling safe. Our safety needs must be satisfied as a prerequisite to our feeling a sense of belonging. We must feel like we belong before gaining esteem. Once we have esteem, we begin to see the big picture. Seeing the big picture empowers us, allowing us to create balanced, fair enterprise level solutions. Only the empowered can see the organization objectively and position it into its place in the world.

As my friend, hotel partner, celebrity and hospitality expert Anthony Melchiorri astutely notes in his sought-after speaking engagements, to satisfy a hotel guest, the hotelier only needs to meet Maslow's first two needs, *physiological* and *safety,* which makes perfect sense. The hotel guest is with you for a relatively short time and requires little more than shelter, a bathroom and the safety of a secure place to sleep. Whether it's a one-star or five-star hotel it's exactly the same, and without those two basic needs being met, you have a no-star hotel!

Anthony, however, would be the first to point-out that when it comes to the hotel's *employees*, the full spectrum of needs would have to be satisfied in order for the employee to feel motivated, cared-for and desirous of happily remaining in your employ for the long term.

The goal of keeping great employees around for the long term was the impetus that led me to discover that combining Bloom's and Maslow's models is the key that unlocks the secret recipe for employee development. The employer needs to feed employees the Maslow stuff in order to help the employees achieve the Bloom stuff. In other words,

An organization needs to satisfy the employee's needs on each of Maslow's levels in order for them to achieve the corresponding progressive level of mastery on Bloom's scale.

Here is how it looks:

MASLOW STUFF FEEDS BLOOM STUFF

Maslow	Bloom
Self-Actualization	Create
Aesthetic	Evaluate
Cognitive	Synthesize
Esteem	Analyze
Belonging	Apply
Safety	Understand
Physiological	Remember

Pretty cool, huh? For example, if a brand-new employee is freezing and doesn't know where the toilet is, (s)he won't be comfortable enough to perform even the easiest, most rote tasks. Once the employee's physiological needs are met, (s)he feels comfortable and take on the next level of challenge on Bloom's pyramid, developing an understanding of the job. To be able to understand the job, the employee must feel safe. Once the employee feels safe, (s)he feels a sense of belonging which will free him/her up to begin applying the skills that have been acquired. And so on and so forth. Makes sense, right?

And here's the other big takeaway we get from combining and viewing Bloom and Maslow's models: SEVEN LEVELS IS ALL THERE

ARE. No more, no less. Therefore, any organization that has more than seven levels is doing something wrong. They are inventing fake levels and having a bunch of fake levels is confusing and wasteful.

Remember my example, way back in Chapter Two, of the company having 12 levels? Here's the answer:

A COMPANY SHOULD NEVER HAVE MORE THAN SEVEN LEVELS: IT IS THE NATURAL ORDER OF THINGS.

Chapter Summary/Key Takeaways

- In order to properly foster employee growth and development, we tapped-into to psychological works of Benjamin Bloom and Abraham Maslow

- Bloom, in his *Taxonomy of Educational Objectives* shows us that for an employee to develop, (s)he must master simpler tasks and concepts before being ready to take on those that are more complex

- Maslow, in his *Hierarchy of Needs* teaches us that the employer must ensure that the employee's innate human needs must be met, from the most basic to the most complex, in order to personally progress towards self-actualization and transcendence.

- When we combine *Bloom's Taxonomy* with *Maslow's Hierarchy,* we unlock an important key to employee development, that employers must meet their employees' innate human needs in order that they may progress both personally and professionally.

- Bloom and Maslow teach us that a company should never have more than seven levels, for that is the natural order of things.

In the next chapter, we will use this key and employ both Bloom's and Maslow's seven levels to unlock your company's potential. We'll help you develop practical competencies, job descriptions and career paths.

Chapter Four: Introduction to Competencies

The Problem with Competencies

Competencies, competencies, competencies. Everybody who fancies themselves an employee development expert talks about them, but I've never seen anyone actually implement them in a practical, useful manner.

I've seen companies spend hundreds of thousands of dollars paying consultants and buying materials, supplies and books about competencies that can be edited down to a couple sheets of 8 ½" x 11" paper.

Seriously…I have seen otherwise seemingly sane people in senior leadership positions sitting around a conference table, *sorting cards* (really expensive cards, I might add) and laying them on the table…cards that say things on them like "action-oriented", "handling paradox" (what?), "intellectual horsepower" (smart, I guess), "personal disclosure" (sounds creepy), "focus on customers" (as opposed to what? Lunch?), "humor" (really?). I could go on and on and on and on.

As a seasoned leader with many years of experience in a fairly wide range of industries, I can honestly say that I've never once, in an interview situation, either asked or been asked how I or the candidate would deal with paradox. I don't know what it is to deal with paradox and I'm frankly a little scared that I probably wouldn't deal with paradox very well. Mostly because I don't know what paradox is, and if confronted with it, I'd probably just run away.

I never did learn what the people did once they were done sorting all those cards, probably because they really didn't do anything with them. They just do the exercise, feel good about their sorting accomplishment, then go on to interview the candidates recruiting presents, asking the same questions they'd always asked in the past, then hired their brother-in-law. Bottom line: I don't think these competencies that people try to identify and define and try to use to hire and develop people are very useful…or even the *real* competencies for that matter.

So, if those aren't the *real competencies*, then what are the real ones, and what the heck are competencies anyways? For our answer, let's consult, once again, with the source and repository of all truth and knowledge, Wikipedia, and see what their contributors have to say about competencies, as follows:

"**Competencies** are the set of demonstrable characteristics and skills that enable, and improve the efficiency or performance of a job… Competencies are also what people need to be successful in their jobs…they include all the related knowledge, skills, abilities, and attributes that form a person's job. This set of context-specific qualities is correlated with superior job performance and can be used as a standard against which to measure job performance as well as to develop, recruit, and hire employees…**they are not the same as job tasks**." I made the last part bold to make the point. We will get to job task-like things soon enough. They will reside on the job description, too, right at the top, we're gonna call them *essential functions* and we'll get to them towards the end.

So, no matter what you hear from all the employee development card-sorters who claim to be experts on competencies, know this…competencies are, once and for all, simply put:

The knowledge, skills and abilities an employee needs to be COMPETENT at their job.

Ya see? *Competencies* has the word *competent* right there in it...right at the beginning. C-O-M-P...well, you probably get it.

So, if *paradox-handling* isn't a real competency, what are the real competencies, and how can we identify them, say, in a police lineup? Well, we have a friend who already did this for us a long time ago, and at the time he probably didn't even know he was doing HR competency work.

Meet Benjamin Bloom, The King of Competencies

Our friend Ben Bloom (and his successors[4]) was kind enough to teach us that there are four and only four flavors of competency categories. Bloom called the *learning domains* - he wasn't hip to competencies back then. These learning domains are exactly what we need and are as follows: *Cognitive, Psychomotor, Affective and Interpersonal*. Let's look at each one in turn.

The *Cognitive* learning domain is KNOWLEDGE-BASED and contains what we *think* and *know*.

---

[4] Bloom's successors expanded on his work – example to follow.

The *Psychomotor* learning domain is ACTION-BASED and contains skills, i.e., what we *do*.

The *Affective* learning domain is EMOTION-BASED and contains what we *feel* and *believe*.

The *Interpersonal* learning domain[5] is RELATIONSHIP-BASED and contains how we *interact in groups*.

These four domains, taken together, are the basis for competency categories that define the *whole employee*. A whole employee is a person, comprised of knowledge, skills, emotions and interpersonal relationships. Within each of these four categories, there are seven progressive levels of mastery, each of which needs to be completed before graduating to the next higher level.

As you will see in the following pages, Bloom (together with Maslow) has given us everything we need to begin building a rubric of competencies that grow into job descriptions, that grow into career paths within job families, that grouped together comprise healthy, stable, productive organizations.

---

[5] As previously stated, Bloom's successors expanded on his work – his original taxonomy did not include an interpersonal domain. It was added by his successors.

Chapter Summary/Key Takeaways

- Heretofore, "experts" have misunderstood and overly complicated *competencies* to the point at which they are no longer useful

- In their purest, simplest and most useful form, competencies can be defined as the knowledge, skills and abilities an employee needs to be COMPETENT at their job

- Bloom (and his successors), in his *taxonomy of learning* has provided us with everything we need to create a rubric of useful competencies, organized into four categories that, taken together, define the whole employee, comprised of knowledge, skills/abilities, feelings/beliefs and interpersonal relationships.

In the next chapter, we will use Bloom's four domains to build a useful rubric of competencies.

Chapter Five: The Four Competencies

As we saw in chapter four, Bloom's four domains map very nicely map to competency categories for knowledge, skills/abilities, feelings/beliefs and interpersonal relationships. The competency categories that naturally flow from Bloom's domains are as follows:

The Cognitive domain becomes JOB FAMILY COMPETENCIES

The Psychomotor domain becomes FUNCTIONAL COMPETENCIES

The Affective domain becomes CORE COMPETENCIES

The Interpersonal domain becomes LEADERSHIP COMPETENCIES

Here's a handy chart that lays them out:

Bloom's Domain	**How/What**	**Competency Category**
Cognitive	Think/Know	Job Family
Psychomotor	Do/Act	Functional
Affective	Believe/Feel	Core
Interpersonal	Interact	Leadership

And here's a definition of each:

JOB FAMILY COMPETENCIES: General occupational knowledge shared by all jobs within a job family.

FUNCTIONAL COMPETENCIES: Technical and professional skills and abilities required to perform a specific job.

CORE COMPETENCIES: The ability to understand, model and promote behaviors that reflect a company's core values to varying degrees.

LEADERSHIP COMPETENCIES: The ability to function and collaborate in team roles as a contributor, professional, manager or leader.

Now pay attention to this next part – it is important! The competencies that you'll be using (either copying or drafting from scratch – but not buying!!) are the key to everything in the lifespan of your employees! I'll say that again, in bold this time. **The competencies are the key to everything in the lifespan of your employees!!**

Competencies are the things that live on your job descriptions and job descriptions are the most important documents you have in your HR arsenal! They are the things that will populate your job postings, so when folks are deciding whether to apply, they'll see these things and say, "hey, I think I can do that."

They're the things that you'll ask about when they interview, so you can see whether they really do have this knowledge and these abilities.

When they convince you to hire them, on their very first day you'll place the job description in front of them (which they already should be familiar with, since they saw the stuff in the job posting, and were asked about it in the interview process - so now they know you were serious about these things) and they will know what is expected of them.

Competencies are the things you'll use to evaluate their performance – you'll track their performance against the expectations set forth in the job description.

They're the things you'll use to coach, discipline and terminate them (for performance) if they fail to meet the expectations laid out in the job description.

And when they want to apply for promotion to the next level up or if you are considering promoting them, you'll first ensure they can do all the stuff on their current job description and evaluate whether you think they are prepared to perform the duties and responsibilities of the next job.

Gone are the days when you look at a job description once and file it away! They should and will become an everyday part of your work life.

Next, we'll examine each competency category, and later we'll map the employee progression up the ladder of Bloom's seven levels. Let's start with the warm and squishy ones first, *core competencies* and *leadership competencies*.

Core Competencies

Core competencies reflect the core values of a specific organization, so each organization will have a different set of them. A company's core values and the competencies that align to them should be shared by all individuals in the organization to varying degrees. Here is, once again, how we define the term. A core competency is:

The ability to understand, model and promote behaviors that reflect a company's core values to varying degrees.

As a place keeper, I have drafted a set that probably applies to a great many types of companies. You may already have a set of company values, but if you don't, these may be a good place to start. In job descriptions, I like to define the term first then lay them out, like this:

CORE COMPETENCIES: The ability to understand, model and promote behaviors that reflect a company's core values to varying degrees.

Coworker, Customer, Mission Orientation and Communication: The ability to demonstrate genuine concern for satisfying one's coworkers, internal and external customers, mindful of the Company's mission (insert mission here) and to freely and constantly communicate information up and down within and without the Company.

Goal-Oriented Quality Performance: The ability to manage and motivate one's own and one's employees' performance, ensuring commitment to exemplary performance and high-quality work by setting clear goals and expectations, and tracking progress, with frequent feedback to allow the celebration of achievements and prompt correction of performance issues.

Empathetic, Culturally Competent Interpersonal Awareness, Communication and Behavior: The ability to notice, anticipate and interpret the needs, concerns and feelings of a diverse network of coworkers, clients and community members, and to evidence this awareness empathetically by communicating and behaving in a respectful and culturally competent manner.

Personal/Company Credibility: Demonstrated concern that one be perceived as an ethical, responsible, reliable and trustworthy representative of the company at all times in all business affairs.

Personal Accountability: The ability to own one's actions, decisions and behaviors and the consequences thereof, and to show respect for others by honoring all personal and professional commitments.

We'll revisit this competency category toward the end as it is in my opinion the most important competency set of all.

Leadership Competencies

Leadership Competencies are often misunderstood. As we discussed in the previous chapter, there are entire books written about leadership competencies and companies pay big bucks to buy systems that focus entirely on identifying and using them, for what, I have absolutely no idea.

As I promised at the beginning, we'll keep things simple here. I have enough trouble recalling what I had for breakfast and remembering to pick my daughter up from tennis let alone remembering the 26-odd competencies that were assigned to me by my AVP of Employee Development (who, by the way, is usually a lousy leader, and who has likely never actually done any actual production work outside of preaching about competencies – remember, *those who can, do, and those who can't, teach!*). This book is about practical solutions – no black boxes here. Okay…back to keeping things simple, practical and useful!

As I inferred earlier, people are often confused about leadership competencies. We're not talking about leaders like General Macarthur. We're taking about something fairly simple, that can be defined as follows:

The ability to function and collaborate in team roles to varying degrees as a contributor, professional, manager or leader.

You'll see from the leadership levels that follow, there are completely different skill sets to *supervising, managing* and *leading*:

LEADERSHIP COMPETENCIES: The ability to function and collaborate in team roles to varying degrees as a contributor, professional, manager or leader.

Level 1: Participates in and provides feedback to a team

Level 2: Participates in teams, discerns appropriate team members, summarizes, communicates alternative opinions considerately

Level 3: Supervises (ability to direct, instruct, monitor and review) *task execution* as a *lead*, and *people/processes* as a *supervisor*

Level 4: Manages (ability to sets goals, plan, implement, monitor and correct) *processes, projects and tasks* as a *lead,* and *people/processes* as a *manager*

Level 5: Leads (ability to influence and guide) large, enterprise level projects and tasks as an *Enterprise SME,* and lead people (strategize, set department goals, align with functional vision) as a *Director or AVP*

Level 6: Enterprise Level Job Family Leadership (ability to set functional vision, aligning with enterprise vision and guide) as a *Fellow or VP* within a specific job family

Level 7: Enterprise Level Leadership (generates enterprise mission, vision, goals culture and values) with other *Top Leaders*

WELCOME TO THE SEVEN LEVEL MODEL!

You see from the leadership level list above that each progressive level has its own competency. Levels one and two show us that, for those levels, leadership competencies are pretty much being led. The other five progressive levels show us the natural progression of leadership development.

Here's another way to look at it. Leadership competencies describe the different roles people have in the leadership process – including being led (participating), supervising (people or processes), managing (people or processes) and leading (people or processes).

That's all the leadership competencies that you need. Yes, one can complicate this further, but why bother needlessly complicate things.

FYI, I have developed an entire rubric of *leadership level criteria*, consisting of many, many words in teeny tiny font, that I have included as an appendix (we keep those sorts of things at the end of the book).

Now that you have some fairly plug-and-play Leadership Competencies (that I've provided and Core Competencies (that you've drafted), we're about half-way there. Next, you'll need to come up with a set of Job Family Competencies and Functional Competencies that track to your families and the specific jobs within each family, respectively.

Job Family Competencies

The first thing you'll have to do is determine what job families you have. In most companies this is a pretty easy process. The list should look something like this:

JOB FAMILIES

Sales	General Administration
IT	Operations
Customer Service	Human Resources
Legal	Finance & Accounting

Once you've identified the job families, you simply have to plug-in the list of general occupational knowledge items that everyone in that job family should possess to varying degrees, e.g., IT people should know computer stuff, HR people should know HR stuff, etc.

Job Family Competencies should start with the term KNOWLEDGE OF…

Here's an extremely simple example from a small company that I worked with recently:

JOB FAMILY COMPETENCIES: General occupational knowledge shared by all jobs within a job family and exercised to varying degrees.

FINANCE

- Knowledge of the principles and practices of finance and accounting

- Knowledge of finance and accounting software

- Knowledge of budgeting principles

- Knowledge of Microsoft Office Suite of software solutions

There could be fewer or more competencies in each of your organization's job families. Only you can define them, but in my experience, you shouldn't have more than half a dozen or so.

Now that you have your job families defined and the knowledge competencies that live in them, we'll need to define and assign the jobs that live in each family. Each of those jobs will have a group of job-specific Functional competencies that define each position.

Functional (Job Specific) Competencies

As we just said in the last paragraph, each job must have a group of job-specific competencies that define the position.

Like job family competencies start with *knowledge of,* functional competencies start with ABILITY TO…

Here's an example of the functional competency set that I helped the same company develop:

FUNCTIONAL COMPETENCIES: Progressive technical and professional skills and abilities required to perform a specific job.

CONTROLLER

- Ability to operate finance and accounting software
- Ability to create and manage budgets, profit and loss statement and balance sheets
- Ability to forecast effectively
- Ability to communicate financial information to non-finance people

And there you have the four flavors of competencies.

Your Best Friend: The Job Description

Now you know that there are four types of competencies and that they live on your job description (or job profile, or whatever you choose to call it at your organization). What else must live on your job description? First let's define the term *Job Description.*

A job description is the document containing the functions, competencies and requirements of a position.

Let's take it from the top. Here's the order I find most useful on job descriptions:

- Top boxes: Job Title, Job Family (Department) Name, Reports-To Position Title, FLSA Exemption Classification, Date Modified

- Essential Functions

- Core Competencies

- Job Family Competencies

- Functional Competencies

- Leadership Competencies

- Legal Stuff (physical requirements, bona fide occupational qualifications, equal opportunity statement, etc.)

We've already covered the competencies and you need to figure-out the legal stuff in your state, city, municipality, so let's spend a moment on *Essential Functions*.

The Society for Human Resources Management (SHRM) describes Essential Functions as the basic job duties that an employee must be able to perform, with or without reasonable accommodation. They are not the same as *functional competencies*, which are the skills and abilities one must possess to perform the *essential functions.* So essential functions are the tasks, duties and responsibility of the position.

Chapter Summary/Key Takeaways

- There are four and only four types of competencies, Core, Leadership, Job Family and Functional, and they live on job descriptions

- The job description is used for everything surrounding a position: recruiting, interviewing, setting expectations, evaluating, promoting, disciplining and termination

- Job description contains everything that defines a position: Competencies, Essential Duties, FLSA Classifications and Legal Disclaimers.

In the next chapter, we'll take a closer look at the seven-level model and help you put it all together both conceptually and visually.

Chapter Six: The Competency-Based, Seven Level Career Development Model

(And the Two Career Paths)

Now you have nearly all the tools you need to build job descriptions that become families of jobs. Those families need to be visible to employees so they can see that there is a future for them in the company AND so they can see the competencies they will need to acquire to progress to the next level.

REMEMBER, THE WHOLE POINT OF THIS IS TO KEEP GOOD EMPLOYEES, AND TO DO THAT YOU NEED TO COMMUNICATE WITH THEM, TREAT THEM RIGHT AND SHOW THEM THERE IS A CAREER PATH WITHIN THE COMPANY!

Seven Levels Revisited

We already know that Our friends Bloom and Maslow showed us that there are four competency types and seven levels. Let's look at each competency type and define the criteria for each level within the seven-level system in order to build the job descriptions and job families that will be visible and offer promotional hope to employees. These are the criteria we will use to evaluate employees and make the determination whether they are ready for promotion to the next level.

Job Family Competencies

Level 1: Recalls general occupational knowledge taught in the course and scope of the job.

Level 2: Comprehends general occupational knowledge.

Level 3: Applies general occupational knowledge.

Level 4: Analyzes occupational knowledge.

Level 5: Synthesizes occupational knowledge and contributes to new systems and models.

Level 6: Develops and evaluates new models.

Level 7: Sets vision and invents/evaluates new systems and models.

Functional Competencies

Level 1: Performs basic duties as instructed. Imitates and copies tasks.

Level 2: Manipulates knowledge to complete tasks.

Level 3: Develops and exhibits precision in task completion.

Level 4: Combines and integrates skills.

Level 5: Displays unconscious mastery to complete tasks.

Level 6: Develops and evaluates new models.

Level 7: Sets vision and invents/evaluates new systems and models.

<u>Leadership Competencies</u>

Level 1: Participates in and provides feedback to a team.

Level 2: Participates in teams, discerns appropriate team members, summarizes and communicates alternative opinions considerately.

Level 3: Ability to direct, instruct, monitor and review task execution as a lead, and people/processes as a supervisor.

Level 4: Ability to set goals, plan, implement, monitor and correct processes, projects and tasks as a subject matter expert, and people as a manager.

Level 5: Influences and guides large, enterprise-level projects and tasks as an enterprise level subject matter expert; Strategizes, sets department goals, aligns with functional vision as a director or associate vice president.

Level 6: Sets functional vision, aligning with enterprise vision and guides as an enterprise level leader.

Level 7: Sets enterprise level leadership vision.

<u>Core Competencies</u>

Level 1: Awareness of organization's culture and values.

Level 2: Participates in organization's culture and values.

Level 3: Values and aligns with organization's culture and values.

Level 4: Fully integrates the organization's culture into work life.

Level 5: Models, influences and motivates organization's culture and values.

Level 6: Embodies and advocates organization's culture and values.

Level 7: Generates the organization's culture and values.

The Two Career Tracks

As we saw in Chapter Three, companies often commit the unforgiveable crime of wrongful promotion, placing perfectly good individual contributors into management position for which (s)he has no aptitude, desire or interest (other than the bigger paycheck) in order to reward and/or retain them. This happens when a highly valuable individual contributor has topped-out in his/her individual career track, so the company promotes the employee to a people-leadership position to keep the talent.

As I pointed-out way back then, the skill set that makes someone an amazing individual contributor (producing quality production output) is completely different from the skill set that makes one an amazing manager (caring for others, team building and the heartfelt desire to see others grow and succeed). Rewarding a star individual contributor with a management position is like rewarding a baby with chainsaw – they'll be frustrated, and they won't know what to do with it, and if they try to use it, they'll probably do an enormous amount of damage.

Job Title Mapping

With each level mapped within the four competency types, the next step is to map the levels to the most traditional job titles within the two career tracks, as follows:

Professional (Individual Contributor) Career Track

Level 1: Trainee

Level 2: Individual Contributor (IC)

Level 3: Lead

Level 4: Subject Matter Expert (SME)

Level 5: Enterprise Level Subject Matter Expert (ESME)

Level 6: Fellow

Level 7: N/A – C-Suite Positions MUST be People Leaders

Management Career Track

Level 1: N/A – There Are No Trainee Level Management Positions

Level 2: N/A – There Are No IC Level Management Positions

Level 3: Supervisor

Level 4: Manager

Level 5: Director/Associate Vice President (AVP)

Level 6: Vice President (VP)/Senior Vice President (SVP)

Level 7: Executive Vice President (EVP) – C-Suite

Having established that there should be equal opportunity for career growth and promotion for both people managers and individual contributors, and having mapped the titles to the levels, here's a handy chart to illustrate the career flow in both tracks:

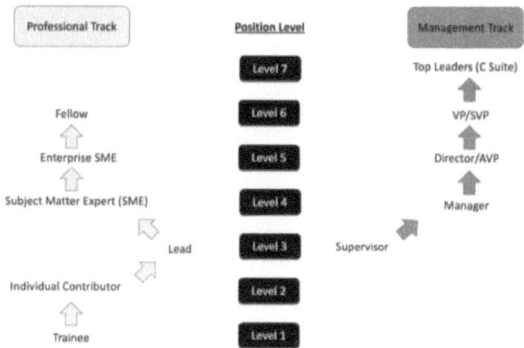

The career flow is for positions within job families, not individuals. That's why there are no level one and two positions in the management track. Every job family necessarily starts with people actually learning and doing jobs. Only when we have satisfied our physiological and safety needs and experience a sense of belonging, we become able to take on the role of actually helping others produce and grow along their career paths.

Please note that folks on the Professional Track can move into Management Track positions and vice versa, but they must have the corresponding Management Track skill set - the tracks are not mutually exclusive.

Now that we understand Bloom and Maslow, defined the four types of competencies, have identified the seven levels and mapped them to job titles, let's put it all together in a handy chart, as follows:

This little chart sums it up pretty nicely (I actually think it's so cool that it should have its own page or a foldout or something).

Experience has shown, however, that the organization, from the top on down, has to be mindful and constantly pay attention to the stuff on the right side or the stuff on the left side won't happen and the company will lose its soul, its best employees and set itself up for miserable failure.

Feed Them or They Won't Grow

Back to the goofy tree analogy once again…apologies. We've already determined that employees need to be fed the Maslow stuff in order to grow and achieve the Bloom stuff, but how do we do that, and who's responsibility is it to do that. The answer is deceptively simple.

We do it through fostering a culture of communication. We feed them with INFORMATION! This is where many, many companies fail. They all say they want transparency and free, open communication up and down the various levels of the company, but this desired communication flow usually gets stuck in the bottleneck of middle management. Lazy managers sit at their desks or in their offices and spend their time trying to look good for their bosses and control the microculture of their department rather than being the coach and conduit that they are meant to be.

In the military, every recruit is given, on day one, a simple set of rules called *general orders*. One of those general orders states as follows:

To repeat all calls more distant from the guard house than my own.

To translate to you civilians, that simply means that if you're in the middle, it is your DUTY to ensure that folks closer to the front line receive the message that you received passed on to them.

To further translate into the language of business, middle managers have a DUTY to be the voice of the employees to their bosses and of their bosses to their subordinates. In my career, I've had countless meetings, written countless memos and made countless videos to communicate programs down the line to employees only to later learn that they never made it down the in front line workers who needed to hear the message. The middle managers simply didn't share the message.

The Companycultural Void

CEO's, executives, department heads, group leaders, directors, managers, supervisors, and basically everyone above level one has the responsibility to ensure that those who report to them (in a supervisory role or in a mentoring role), or simply who sit below them anywhere on the company ladder regardless of job family, are given *information*, praise, recognition and whatever else they need to progress along the Needs Hierarchy, or they will live in an informational and *companycultural void* (yes, I made that term up).

Without receiving the information that is meant for them, an employee's motivation and therefore career will stall, and they'll get bored and/or disenchanted, and start looking elsewhere. This is a cross-functional, bottom-to-top, entire company thing! We all simply need to take care of each other and show that caring through complete and constant communication!

Everyone must also be an ambassador for the company's culture, and that culture MUST be one of praise, recognition and communication.

Example: if a level 4 person in sales notices something that an IT coordinator did something great to help them and make their job easier, it is their DUTY to praise them and thank them for making the company a better place. Doing so will give the IT kid the confidence and esteem that (s)he needs to keep striving to do better, progress and help the company succeed.

So how do we avoid the companycultural void and create a culture of communication? It's not as hard as it sounds, actually, and it begins with *hiring the right people* at the beginning and *only keeping and promoting those that exhibit and embody the company's culture and values*. More on this in the last chapter.

Show Them the Way

The competency-based career development program that I've outlined will only succeed if employees can actually SEE that there is a job path and therefore a future for them in the organization.

There's an old HR adage that states *a compensation program is only as valuable as its being communicated,* meaning employees won't appreciate the value of their total compensation unless they are aware of it. A total comp package is much more than a paycheck – it includes the value of paid time off (sick time, vacation time) health benefits, retirement contribution matches, etc., and employees won't appreciate the total value of their compensation unless we provide them with a total compensation statement regularly – their supervisor/manager should personally go over the statement with them to ensure the employee understands and appreciates it.

Likewise, career paths are only as valuable as their being visible, communicated and understood by everyone. Job descriptions, competencies and job paths should not live in a black hole within the companycultural void!

The org chart is your friend. Post the damn thing on your wall and celebrate it! Every employee, from day one, should be able to see where (s)he lives on it, getting perspective as to how their position fits in and contributes to the organization as a whole. The employee deserves to see and know where (s)he can go if (s)he does a good job and develops competencies and grows, both within their current job family and in other job families. Other job families? Really? As a manager, I may lose my awesome employee to another department? The answer is yes.

I'm now going to use the term *ownership*, but not in a way that would violate the Thirteenth Amendment to the US Constitution:

THE COMPANY OWNS THE EMPLOYEE, NOT THE DEPARTMENT.

Yes – sometimes an employee realizes that their talents, competencies translate to a different job family where they want to be, and companies have to allow the employee to move into different department in order to retain them. People do a better job at things they enjoy doing, so we have to let them follow their own heart and move into other positions for which they are qualified. It's better to keep the talent than lose them to another company. Managers have to let go and realize that the employee is not quitting them, but merely finding their own path.

How do we ensure that managers foster a culture of communication and free movement? Again – hire folks who think like that from the start and constantly foster that culture.

The next and final chapter (YAY) will address this very issue from a very good place to start…at the very beginning.

Chapter Summary/Key Takeaways

- Job descriptions are an organization's most important HR tool

- Job descriptions, which contain Competencies, Essential Duties, FLSA Classifications and Legal Disclaimers, live on seven distinct organizational levels

- Each level contains its own criteria that must be satisfied in order for an employee to occupy a position on that level

- There are two separate, equivalent career paths for people managers and individually contributing professionals, and employees can cross the divide between them if qualified

- Everyone in the organization has a sacred duty to communicate up and down to avoid the companycultural void and help everyone else achieve their career goals

Chapter Seven: Before the Seven Levels:

Hire Right

So, there you have it - a complete seven level, competency-based career development model to help you recruit, train, evaluate, motivate, promote, correct, discipline and yes, terminate employees. But before a new employee starts his or her journey at your company, they first have to get hired. This is where you have the most power and you absolutely have to do this right.

You are the gatekeeper, the keeper of the keys, and nobody, absolutely nobody gets invited in unless they pass the test!

What's the test? Well, as I stated in Chapter Five, core competencies are the most important competencies of all. They are the things that track to your company's culture and values, and your culture and values must be guarded like the hope diamond, or a really nice sweater that your daughter has her eye on, or the last piece of cake, or your good name and reputation. This is where the language gets colorful – real life stuff.

Hire for Cultural Fit

From the first time we peek at a candidate's resume, we need to be keenly observing for cultural fit. When we interview the candidate, the most important thing to look for is cultural fit. When the three or four other people (hopefully from different departments) interview the candidate, they need to be told that, most importantly, they are looking for cultural fit.

One of the most important things I learned in law school was towards the end, and it had absolutely nothing whatsoever to do with law. I was sitting through an excruciatingly painful seminar on how to interview for a job at a law firm. The panel consisted of alumni, some of whom had recently graduated and some old timers who just enjoyed imparting their wisdom to future attorneys.

Of course, all the bright, fresh, young lawyers told us how to dress and to highlight our work ethic, clerking experience and law school accomplishments. They went on and on, probably trying to impress us, the folks whose seats they occupied a year or two earlier, and I was ready to walk out. A beer was sounding good to me. But then the old timer on the panel spoke up and said something that completely changed how I looked at interviewing for a job.

He said, "Listen. The lawyer who's interviewing you doesn't give a shit what you're wearing, or whether you were on law review or won a prize for moot court or clerked for a federal judge. He wants to know if he likes you and whether he'll either enjoy or hate seeing you every morning and working with you every day. **He wants to know whether you're an asshole**." Apologies for the colorful language, but I wanted the quote to be accurate. We'll use *jerk* going forward!

I loved this guy. He spoke the truth. It was like the sky opened and the angels said that. To put it in organizationally correct parlance, people like to work with nice people. People like to work with people who share their views and outlook. And you only have one chance to weed-out the culturally incompatible.

BEFORE YOU HIRE THEM.

I know I'm preaching to the choir here, but once you hire someone, onboard them, put them through new employee orientation, train them, equip them and get them started, it is extremely difficult and expensive to get rid of them.

So, do whatever it takes to weed-out the jerks before you hire someone.

Fire for Cultural Incompatibility

When the odd jerk does slip through the cracks (and it happens to all of us), do yourself a favor and fire them immediately. And always remember this: we don't fire people, they fire themselves! Sometimes they're harder to spot than *an italics period.*

Oftentimes, bad employees "manage up", which means, for those of you unfamiliar with the term, the employee acts like the model of a perfect employee to their bosses and their boss's bosses, but treats everyone below them with distain, disrespect and dismissiveness. This can go on for years. The jerk's employees keep quitting or transferring out of their department and either nobody tracks or notices it, or the jerk has an excuse ("he couldn't handle the pace, pressure, whatever).

Allowing a culturally incompatible employee to stay one day longer than you absolutely have to is like inviting a cancer into your company. It spreads, infects an enormous number of people and its ill effects can be felt for years after the bad apple has moved on to infect another firm.

I've been frustrated many times in my career with people leaders who hire the wrong person then, when they realize this, refuse to fire them. I'm not a fan of progressive discipline or performance improvement plans or behavioral coaching. Here are two mantras that I absolutely live by, and they have served me well…

You can change what people do but you cannot change who they are.

You can't coach *jerk* out of someone.

Good people tend to stay good and jerks will always be jerks. Hire a grump and I guarantee they won't be cheerful on their first, or their last, day.

Wow! You made it through the book. Congratulations. I sure hope the ideas I presented were eye-opening helpful. They were meant to be.

Chapter Summary/Key Takeaways

- Hire nice people

- When you make a mistake and hire a jerk, fire them immediately

- You can change what people do but not who they are

- You can't coach jerk out of someone

Epilogue

Once again, I'd like to thank you, dear reader, for purchasing my little book. I hope, from the bottom of my Irish American heart that what I've shared will help you and your company. I still find it crazy that one statement made by a dearly departed psychologist to an HR guy could lead to a new HR model, but I'm sure glad that it did.

I know that I said, WAY back in the Introduction, that consultants are a waste of money and all they really want to do is take your money and extend their consultancy for as long as possible, and I do believe that with all my heart.

However, if you like my approach and would like to spend a few bucks and a couple days with a very enthusiastic, likeable HR fellow, I'd be happy to come to your company and spend a little time with you talking about HR stuff and getting this model set up. It'll only cost you a plane ticket, a couple of nights in a hotel, a few sandwiches and a modest fee. My email is: tlemmis@gmail.com

Acknowledgments

I'd like to thank all my former bosses who shaped my views on HR, management and business. The amazing ones and horrible ones taught me much. I'm also grateful to the following people who, whether they knew it or not, contributed to the book:

- Robert Ferguson, Esq. & Jack Kemp, Esq.

- The Molina Brothers, John, JD and Mario, MD

- Dr. Larry Lewis, dearly departed psychologist

- Bob Gordon, Kevin Davis, Jon Heiman and David Telling

- Chief Phil Gonshak, Seal Beach Police Department

- Steve Goodling, Long Beach Convention & Visitors Bureau

Finally, thank you to my beautiful wife, Gjusta and our three children, James, Charles & Sarah. You suffer me every day - I'm grateful and I love you all so much for it.

About the Author

Todd J. Lemmis, JD, is a Navy veteran, musician, lawyer, businessperson, HR guy and impact investment/developer. He holds a Bachelor of Arts degree in philosophy from UCLA and a Juris Doctorate from Southwestern Law School.

He lives in Long Beach, California with his cute wife and three above average children. He's active in his community and sits on the boards of the Long Beach Convention and Visitor's Bureau, The Downtown Long Beach Alliance, The Long Beach Public Library Foundation and The Seal Beach Police League. He participates as a member of the Long Beach Police Officers Association (Honorary) and Fire Department Civilian Recruit Interview Panel. He's also a member of the Society of The Friendly Sons of St. Patrick, the US Navy Musicians Association and the Society for Human Resource Management.

In his spare time, he likes to cook, entertain, play the saxophone and design wallets. He also likes cats and invented a punctuation mark: www.lettersign.squarespace.com

Appendices

The appendices that follow are an example of the criteria that can be used to define the levels and to determine whether an employee is ready to execute the duties and responsibilities of each.

Please note there are no criteria for level 7. Transcendence is extremely difficult, nearly impossible, to define. It's like the late Justice Potter Stewart's definition of obscenity in the Supreme Court's 1964 *Jacobellis v. Ohio* opinion, wherein he stated, "I know it when I see it."

I hope you find them useful and when you find brilliance, kindness and potential in a truly gifted candidate or employee, I hope you see it.

APPENDIX A

LEVEL	CRITERIA							
	CRITERIA	LEADERSHIP COMPETENCIES	CORE COMPETENCIES CULTURAL ALIGNMENT	EDUCATION	RELEVANT EXPERIENCE	MIN TIME IN CURRENT POSITION	SUPERVISORY EXPERIENCE	SPAN OF CONTROL
Level 1 (Entry Level Individual Contributor only)	Recalls general occupational knowledge taught in course and scope of job. Performs basic duties as instructed. Imitates and copies tasks.	Participates in and provides feedback to a team.	Awareness of company culture and values.	HS diploma or GED	0-1 Year	N/A	N/A	N/A
Level 2 (Individual Contributor only)	Comprehends general occupational knowledge, manipulates knowledge to complete tasks.	Participates in teams, discerns appropriate team members, summarizes, and communicates alternative options considerably.	Participation in company culture and values.	Associate's degree or equivalent combination of education and work experience	1-3 Years	1 Year	N/A	Individual Projects
Level 3 (Lead/Supervisor)	Applies general occupational knowledge and develops precision.	Ability to direct, instruct, implement, monitor, and review task execution as a lead, and people/processes as a supervisor.	Value and align with company culture and values.	Associate's degree or equivalent combination of education and work experience	3-4 Years	18 Months	MGMT TRACK: Developing, not required (aptitude and awareness)	MGMT TRACK: Small groups within a department
								INDIV TRACK: Small projects
Level 4 (SME/Manager)	Analyzes occupational knowledge and combines and integrates skills.	Ability to set goals, plan, processes, projects, and tasks as a SME, and people as a manager.	Fully integrate company culture and values into worklife.	Bachelor's degree or equivalent combination of education and work experience	5-6 Years	2 Years	PROF TRACK: N/A	PROF TRACK: Medium or multiple small projects
								MGMT TRACK: 1 Year - Proficient
								MGMT TRACK: Department
Level 5 (Enterprise SME/ Director/AVP)	Synthesizes occupational knowledge, creating new systems and models. Displays unconscious mastery to complete tasks.	Influences and guides large, enterprise-level projects and tasks as an Ent. SME. Strategizes, sets department goals, aligns with functional vision as a Dir/AVP.	Model, influence, and motivate company culture and values.	Master's degree or equivalent combination of education and work experience	7+ Years	PROF TRACK: N/A (Renowned expert in field)	INDIV TRACK: N/A	INDIV TRACK: Large or enterprise level projects
						PROF TRACK: 2 Years		
						MGMT TRACK: 2 Years	MGMT TRACK: 3 Years - Role Model	MGMT TRACK: Business Unit
Level 6 (Fellow/VP/SVP)	Develops and evaluates new systems and models.	Sets functional vision, aligning with enterprise vision and guides as an enterprise level leader.	Embodies, advocates and shadows company culture and values.	Master's degree or equivalent combination of education and work experience	10+ Years	MGMT TRACK: 3 Years	MGMT TRACK: 5 Years - True Leader	MGMT TRACK: Multiple business units
							INDIV TRACK: N/A	INDIV TRACK: Multiple enterprise level projects

Supervisor Level Requirements

Strategy	Leadership	Specialized Knowledge	Decision Making	Problem Solving	Authority	Collaboration
Supervisor's input on the impact of strategic changes to his/her team's work product may be solicited.	Supervisor assigns tasks and provides oversight for daily activities of employees. Typically, subordinate roles are routine in nature. Provides advice on how to handle routine tasks, processes, and deliver work product in a timely manner. May step in to assist with problem solving. Provides regular coaching, feedback, and recommendations on training and basic developmental opportunities for assigned work group. Shared responsibility to hire and terminate assigned employees.	Supervisor displays proficiency in a sub-discipline to identify and remove obstacles to productivity and solve problems within assigned area, including for assigned team.	Supervisor, within purview of pre-determined work assignments, has discretion to determine assignment of tasks and processes in support of specific objectives and established goals. Exercises judgment within pre-determined processes, policies, and guidelines. Develops and administers schedules and workforce coverage. May have limited budget responsibility. Work is reviewed and measured for successful completion and delivery of work product to meet team function's goals and objectives.	Supervisor works on problems in routine or similar situations that are typically solved by simple choice among learned alternatives. Resolves day-to-day problems using generally defined processes. Follows processes and operational policies in selecting methods and techniques for obtaining solutions. May document processes that support decision making.	Supervisor determines workforce coverage for assigned work production including employee schedules, daily assignments, and overtime. Interprets and executes on policies and procedures for assigned team. May recommend modifications to operating policies and procedures.	Supervisor frequently interacts with customers, and/or functional peers. May interact with middle management on occasion. Interactions normally involve routine matters specific to assigned team. May be regular participant or even lead small, cooperative efforts among members of a project team.

89

Manager Level Requirements

Strategy	Leadership	Specialized Knowledge	Decision Making	Problem Solving	Authority	Collaboration
Manager's input may be solicited during strategic planning in relation to his/her team's ability to operationalize and deliver on forthcoming strategic direction. May also provide key insights into components of strategy as relevant to his/her team.	Manager assigns work and provides oversight for work product of employees. Subordinate roles may be routine in nature or have a degree of discretion and independent decision making. Advises on how to manage and deliver work product in a timely manner. May assist with critical problem solving. Provides regular coaching, feedback, and recommendations on developmental (including relevant training) opportunities. May assist subordinate supervisors with complex or challenging people management activities. Full accountability to hire and terminate across assigned team.	Manager displays strong proficiency in a discipline to identify and remove obstacles to productivity. Exercises judgment within general policies, guidelines, and practices in selecting methods and techniques for determining solutions to said goals and objectives. Develops schedules and administers performance requirements. May have some budget responsibility. Work is reviewed and measured based on completion, delivery and adequacy in meeting functional area's objectives and schedules.	Manager receives pre-determined work assignments with specific objectives and established goals. Exercises judgment within general policies, guidelines, and practices in selecting methods and techniques for determining solutions to said goals and objectives. Develops schedules and administers performance requirements. May have some budget responsibility. Work is reviewed and measured based on completion, delivery and adequacy in meeting functional area's objectives and schedules.	Manager works on problems that are generally routine or similar situations that are likely solved by choosing among learned, but situationally-driven alternatives. Most assignments, and often resolves day-to-day problems using generally defined processes and following policies and procedures that typically affect small portions of business units. May create new or variant solutions for unusual situations encountered.	Manager determines workforce coverage for assigned team including employee schedules, daily overtime. Interprets, implements, and executes on defined processes and following policies and procedures that typically affect small portions of business units. May take lead on reviewing and making recommendations for modifying operating policies and procedures.	Manager frequently interacts with subordinates, customers, and/or functional peers. May interact with mid-level, and occasionally senior level, management. Interactions normally involve matters between functional areas. Often leads cooperative efforts among members of a project team.

Director Level Requirements

Strategy	Leadership	Specialized Knowledge	Decision Making	Problem Solving	Authority	Collaboration
Director participates in complex (non-routine, non-administrative) a business unit's strategic planning function, typically planning through subordinate management roles. May participate in interpreting strategic planning for organizational business. Develops strategic plan for function, including strategies and establishing operational objectives, strategic plans and ensures their achievement. Decisions may effect entire organization.	Director leads a seasoned proficiency to provide deep understanding of underlying principles/ theories/policies and leadership perspective to a broad group of areas/fields. Able to easily communicate in clear, understandable terms across the enterprise. Sought as a leader for chosen field/disciplines within the organization and possibly externally.	Director displays seasoned proficiency to provide deep understanding of underlying principles/ theories/policies and leadership perspective to a broad group of areas/fields. Able to easily communicate in clear, understandable terms across the enterprise. Sought as a leader for chosen field/disciplines within the organization and possibly externally.	Director receives assignments in the form of mid- to long-term plans and strategies for the business unit and enterprise. Exercises notable judgment within broadly defined policies, principles, or practices and evaluation of impact across major functional areas of the business. Develops action plans and ensures schedules meet budgets and corporate requirements. Work results are reviewed and measured for desired results from a mid- to long-term perspective.	Director works on abstract problems in variable situations that typically require with sharing innovative level management concerning several functional areas or solutions to achieve broad organizational issues. policies and Interactions normally intangible factors. involve negotiations Directs the on difficult matters. resolution of Influences policy complex making. Expected to problems that influence or persuade have impact senior level leaders beyond own area. regarding matters of Participates in significance. development of Leverages corporate relationships with techniques, and key internal/external modifications to clients to identify company-wide emerging business policies. needs.	Director regularly determines what needs to be done and is involved with sharing innovative level management concerning several functional areas or organizational issues. Interactions normally involve negotiations on difficult matters. Influences policy making. Expected to influence or persuade senior level leaders regarding matters of significance. Participates in development of corporate techniques, and modifications to company-wide policies.	Director regularly interacts with customers, senior and/or executive level management concerning several functional areas or organizational issues. Interactions normally involve negotiations on difficult matters. Influences policy making. Expected to influence or persuade senior level leaders regarding matters of significance. Leverages relationships with key internal/external clients to identify emerging business needs.

Associate Vice President Level Requirements

Strategy	Leadership	Specialized Knowledge	Decision Making	Problem Solving	Authority	Collaboration
AVP participates in a business unit's strategic planning process, interpreting organizational business strategies and establishing strategic plans and objectives. Decisions may have noteworthy effect on entire organization.	AVP leads and directs 2 or more complex (non-routine, non-administrative) functions, typically through subordinate management roles. Participates in strategic planning for the business unit. Develops strategic plan for assigned functions, including operational objectives, and ensures their achievement. Provides regular coaching and development to assigned people managers and facilitates achievement of team goals, as needed. Designs and implements development plans at the function level to build talent base and long-term individual growth for extended team. Full accountability to hire and terminate, including approval of subordinate management team's decisions, across functions.	AVP displays seasoned proficiency to provide deep understanding of underlying principles/theories/ policies and degree of judgment within broadly defined policies, principles, or practices and evaluation of impact across major functional areas of the business, possibly at an enterprise level. Develops action plans and ensures schedules meet business unit requirements. Work results are reviewed and measured for desired results from a relatively long-term perspective.	AVP receives assignments in the form of long-term plans and strategies for the business unit and enterprise. Exercises a large degree of judgment within broadly defined policies, principles, or practices and evaluation of impact across major functional areas of the business, possibly at an enterprise level. Develops action plans and ensures schedules meet business unit requirements. Work results are reviewed and measured for desired results from a relatively long-term perspective.	AVP works on abstract problems in complex, variable situations that typically require complex analysis, interpretation, and/or evaluation of intangible factors. Directs the resolution of complex organizational problems that have impact beyond own area. Leads and participates in leadership role in designing and launching company-wide policies.	AVP consistently determines what needs to be done and is involved with sharing industry leading, innovative solutions to achieve goals and objectives. Establishes organizational policies in a major segment of the company. May take a leadership role in designing and launching company-wide policies.	AVP consistently interacts with important stakeholders, including senior and executive level management concerning organizational opportunities & issues. Interactions normally involve negotiations of complex, mission critical matters. Proven ability to influence policy making. Proven ability to influence or persuade senior level leaders regarding matters of organizational significance. Leverages relationships with key internal/external clients to identify emerging business needs.

Vice President Level Requirements

Strategy	Leadership	Specialized Knowledge	Decision Making	Problem Solving	Authority	Collaboration
VP leads a business unit's strategic planning, and/or a mission critical function for the enterprise, typically through interpreting organizational business strategies and establishing cross-functionally across the organization strategic plans and objectives. Decisions may have large effect on entire organization.	VP leads and directs 3 or more complex (non-routine, non-administrative) functions provide deep understanding of plans and strategies for the business unit and enterprise. Participates in strategic planning for the business unit and possibly broad group of areas/fields. Communicates ably across the enterprise, easily influencing decisions regarding assigned areas of expertise. Looked to as a thought leader both within and outside of the organization. Develops strategic plan for assigned function, including operational objectives, and their achievement. Provides regular coaching and development opportunities to assigned people managers emphasizing achievement of function(s) goals through leadership team. Designs and implements developmental plans at the function and basic organization level to build talent base and long-term individual growth for extended team.	VP displays seasoned proficiency to provide deep understanding of plans and strategies for the business unit and enterprise. Exercises wholly independent and leadership theories/policies judgment within and principles/broadly defined underlying policies, practices, or practices and evaluation of impact across major functional areas of the business and at the enterprise level. Develops and ensures budgets and schedules meet business unit requirements. Work results are reviewed and measured for desired results from a long-term perspective.	VP determines and sets the direction for business unit based upon long-term problems and strategies that typically require complex, time sensitive analysis. interpretation, and evaluation of intangible factors. Leads resolution of enterprise critical, complex problems that have impact beyond own area. Is viewed as a consistent leader of corporate development of methods, techniques, and evaluation criteria for projects, programs, and people.	VP works on abstract, critical problems in prioritizing what needs to be accomplished within assigned business unit, in support of enterprise-wide objectives, and takes lead on mission critical ability to influence objectives within business unit or smaller undertakings at the enterprise level.	VP takes leadership position in prioritizing what senior and executive level management concerning organizational opportunities & issues. Interactions normally involve negotiations of leading edge, mission critical matters. Proven ability to influence critical policies. Proven ability to influence or persuade senior level leaders and key customers regarding matters of organizational significance. Leverages relationships with key internal/external clients to identify emerging business needs and acts upon.	VP primary interactions are with key customers, senior and executive level management concerning organizational opportunities & issues. Interactions normally involve negotiations of leading edge, mission critical matters. Proven ability to influence critical policies. Proven ability to influence or persuade senior level leaders and key customers regarding matters of organizational significance. Leverages relationships with key internal/external clients to identify emerging business needs and acts upon.

Senior Vice President Level Requirements

Strategy	Leadership	Specialized Knowledge	Decision Making	Problem Solving	Authority	Collaboration
SVP provides input on enterprise-wide strategic planning and leads assigned business units' strategic planning process. Leads design of business strategies, soliciting subordinate leadership team's assistance in establishing strategic plans and objectives. Finalized strategies may have significant effect on entire organization.	SVP leads and directs a key strategic, externally visible function(s) for the enterprise. Manages through subordinate people managers Participates in strategic planning for the enterprise. Develops theories/policies principles/ underlying strategic plan for assigned business unit(s) and delegates planning of operational objectives to people management team. Facilitates team's effectiveness at senior levels of organization to ensure effective achievement of goals and objectives. Provides coaching and developmental opportunities to own leadership team. Designs and implements strategic development plans at the enterprise level to build talent base and long-term individual growth for extended team.	SVP displays seasoned proficiency to provide deep understanding of underlying principles/ theories/policies plans and strategies for the business unit and enterprise. Communicates ably with top management and across all levels of the enterprise, easily influencing strategic decisions both within and without own areas of expertise. Looked to as a strategic leader within the organization and as a visible champion of the enterprise externally.	SVP designs and sets the direction for a large business unit or noticeable portion of the enterprise based upon long-term complex plans and strategies for the business unit and enterprise. Exercises wholly independent judgment within broadly defined policies, principles, or practices and evaluation of impact at the enterprise level. Develops and ensures budgets and schedules meet corporate requirements. Work results are reviewed and measured for desired results from long-term perspective.	SVP works on most pressing enterprise-wide problems that require timeliness, accomplished complex problem solving, relationship management, and takes lead on mission critical objectives.	SVP takes leadership position in prioritizing what needs to be accomplished enterprise-wide opportunities concerning organizational objectives and concerns. Interactions focused on negotiations of future business opportunities and directions. Proven ability to influence with this level of defined internal and external current and future partners.	SVP primary interactions are with key customers, executive level management, and target business

94

www.ingramcontent.com/pod-product-compliance
Lightning Source LLC
Chambersburg PA
CBHW031446210526
45464CB00005B/2345